Lincoln Township Library

W9-AKE-867

COOKING THE
EAST AFRICAN
WAY

Copyright © 2002 by Lerner Publications Company

All rights reserved. International copyright secured. No part of this book may be reproduced, stored in a retrieval system, or transmitted in any form or by any means—electronic, mechanical, photocopying, recording, or otherwise—without the prior written permission of Lerner Publications Company, except for the inclusion of brief quotations in an acknowledged review.

Lerner Publications Company
A division of Lerner Publishing Group
241 First Avenue North
Minneapolis, MN 55401 U.S.A.

Website address: www.lernerbooks.com

Library of Congress Cataloging-in-Publication Data

Montgomery, Bertha Vining.
    Cooking the East African way / by Bertha Vining Montgomery and Constance Nabwire—Rev. & expanded.
       p.   cm. — (Easy menu ethnic cookbooks)
    Includes index.
    ISBN: 0-8225-4164-5 (lib. bdg. : alk. paper)
    1. Cookery, African—Juvenile literature. 2. Africa—Social life and customs—Juvenile literature. [1. Cookery, African. 2. Africa, East—Social life and customs.] I. Nabwire, Constance R. II. Title. III. Series.
TX725.A4 M65   2002
641.59676—dc21   00-013231

Manufactured in the United States of America
1 2 3 4 5 6 – JR – 07 06 05 04 03 02

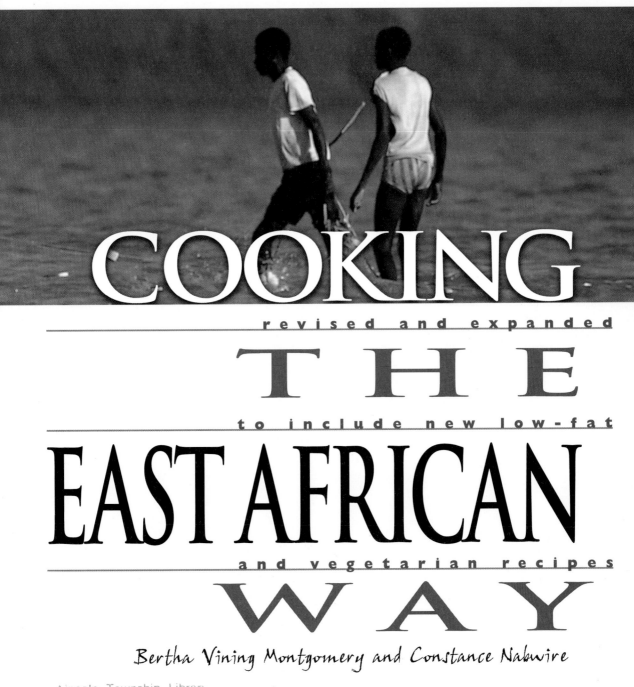

easy menu ethnic cookbooks

COOKING

revised and expanded

THE

to include new low-fat

EAST AFRICAN

and vegetarian recipes

WAY

Bertha Vining Montgomery and Constance Nabwire

Lincoln Township Library
2099 W. John Beers Rd.
Stevensville, MI 49127
429-9575

Lerner Publications Company • Minneapolis

Contents

Introduction

East Africa, home of grass savannas (plains with few trees), elephants, and safaris, is the Africa often featured in movies and books. Most of the countries that make up East Africa—Ethiopia, Eritrea, Somalia, Kenya, Tanzania, and Uganda—border the Red Sea, the Indian Ocean, or Lake Victoria. Great Britain once controlled most of this part of Africa, so for a long time, British cuisine has been the food of choice. East Indian immigrants to the region introduced East Africans to Indian foods such as chapatis (Indian flat bread), pilau (a rice and meat dish), samusas (potato-stuffed pastries), and curry (a spicy meat and vegetable dish), which appear regularly on East African tables. Traditional East African cooking features meat stews flavored with chili peppers served on the side.

People in Uganda and Kenya enjoy greens steamed with coconut milk, tomatoes, and onions. (Recipe on page 41.)

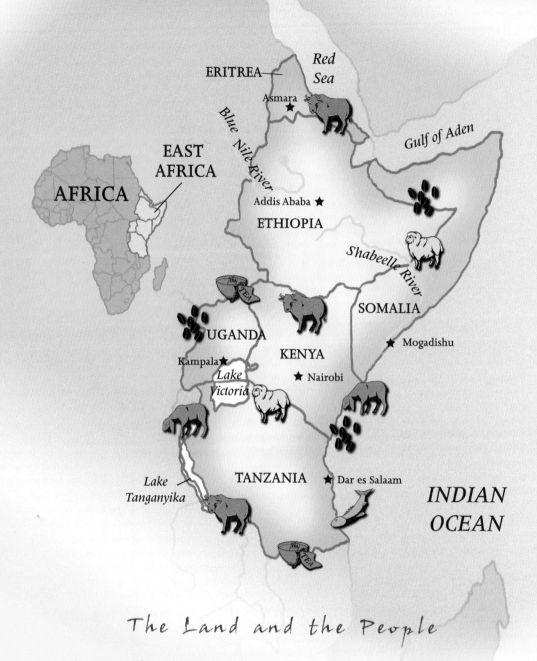

AFRICA

EAST
AFRICA

ERITREA

Red
Sea

Asmara ★

Blue Nile River

Gulf of Aden

Addis Ababa ★

ETHIOPIA

Shabeelle River

SOMALIA

UGANDA

KENYA

Kampala ★

Lake
Victoria

★ Nairobi

Mogadishu ★

Lake
Tanganyika

TANZANIA

Dar es Salaam ★

INDIAN
OCEAN

The Land and the People

The land of East Africa is varied, featuring soaring mountains and steep valleys, thick forests, barren deserts, lush seacoasts, and fertile highlands. It contains the highest mountain in Africa—Mount Kilimanjaro—which is located in northeastern Tanzania. Lake

Victoria, the second largest lake in the world, lies on the borders of Uganda, Kenya, and Tanzania.

Because the equator runs through the countries of Kenya and Uganda, it is not surprising that most of East Africa is hot year-round. There are also highland areas that stay quite cool—often below 50°F—as well as mountains that are tall enough to be snow-capped. Rainfall is uneven across this part of Africa. Some areas have seasons of nearly constant rain, while others receive almost none at all. Drought has been a problem, especially in Ethiopia, where lack of rain has led to serious food shortages.

Africans, Europeans, Middle Easterners, and Asians all call East Africa home. Although most East Africans are black, they are divided into hundreds of ethnic groups, each with its own language and traditions.

The lives of East Africans vary greatly depending on whether they make their homes in the city or in the country. Those who live in cities are more likely to have modern conveniences such as electricity, stoves, and televisions. East Africans who reside in the country live very much as their ancestors did. They usually live in villages with relatives and other people of the same ethnic group. While some villages have houses made of modern materials such as cement and metal, many people still live in houses made of clay or dried mud with roofs of grass or palm leaves. In the majority of these villages, homes do not have running water or electricity.

Most East Africans who live in villages are farmers who work just outside the village on large plantations that grow crops such as coffee or tea. East African women spend their days caring for their children and gardening to feed the family. At harvesttime, the women cart any extra food to the village market. These open-air markets are places where people meet to talk with friends, buy fruits and vegetables, and shop for cloth and other handmade goods.

Women also prepare the family meals. Because most East African cooks don't have electricity or running water, the traditional meals they make take a lot of time. Women must gather firewood and carry water in buckets from a local well. Cooks still use a traditional cooking tool called a mortar and pestle. A pestle is a club-shaped utensil that is used with a mortar (a sturdy bowl) to grind grain into flour or to pound foods, such as plantains. The women may also grind flour on a curved stone. East Africans, especially those who live in villages, still cook over a fire in outdoor kitchens.

Because food is sometimes scarce, East African cooks have learned to work with whatever they have. African dishes are versatile enough that if a certain ingredient is not available, it is always possible to substitute another or leave it out.

The Food

East Africans usually eat only two meals per day, one around lunchtime and the other in the evening. But they snack all day long. A snack might be a piece of chapati, roasted or fried plantains, or samusas. In the cities, these and other snack foods are sold on the street. It is unusual to eat something sweet for a snack, except perhaps for a piece of fruit or a doughnut.

Because very few people have refrigeration, the cooking of East Africa is based on fresh foods. In the villages, people grow all of their own fruits and vegetables in small gardens. Although the people who live in the cities may have refrigeration and rely somewhat on canned foods, they are still likely to visit the market every day for fresh fruits and vegetables.

Farmers grow wheat, rice, sweet potatoes, plantains, and green vegetables such as spinach. In coastal areas, fish is added to soups and stews. Meat and poultry are sometimes scarce. One reason that soups and stews are such staples in East Africa is that they make a little meat stretch to feed many people. Many meals don't contain meat. Chicken is usually saved for guests or special occasions. Meat, poultry, and fish are usually served fresh, although they are sometimes preserved by smoking or drying.

For a long time, it was difficult to find East African cookbooks, because favorite recipes of British settlers were often featured instead. This may have been because most East African cooks do not follow written recipes when cooking. Recipes have long been committed to memory and passed down from generation to generation.

A woman in Tanzania uses rhythmic strokes to grind grain into a fine powder that will eventually be made into bread.

A market in Kenya displays pineapples, mangoes, and citrus fruits, which thrive in the country's warmer areas.

The recipes in this book were collected from women from different countries all over East Africa and then adapted to American measuring standards. A few of the recipes have been changed slightly to suit Western tastes. For the most part, however, the recipes are authentic. Once you have had a taste of East African cooking, you might try varying the meats and vegetables, making up your own combinations.

Holidays and Festivals

Independence day and religious holidays give East Africans plenty of opportunities to celebrate throughout the year. On these special days, East Africans splurge on more expensive foods, such as lamb and other meats, to make meals something to remember.

Many East African countries, including Kenya and Somalia, were once British colonies. Each year these countries host a big party, featuring parades and special meals, to celebrate their independence. December 12, 1963, was the day Kenya gained its independence. Each year, Kenyans travel to their home village to celebrate the day with family and friends. In big cities like Nairobi and Mombasa, parades wind down the streets. Traditional dancers and musicians dress in elaborate costumes and entertain the crowd. Since 1960, Somalians have celebrated Harnemo (Independence Day) on June 26. Everyone has the day off from work and school. They dress in colorful clothes, wear gold jewelry, and dance away the day. Foods such as rice, beef, camel, goat, fish, and halwud, a dessert made with ginger and sugar, make Harnemo a holiday to look forward to.

Religious holidays and festivals occur throughout the year in East Africa. In Somalia, where most of the population is Muslim, Islamic holidays such as Ramadan, Eid al-Fitr, and Molit are important. Ramadan is the holiest month in the Islamic calendar. It was during this time that Muhammad, the Islamic prophet, received his first messages from Allah, or God. Muslims honor Allah during the month of Ramadan by fasting (refusing to eat or drink) from daybreak until sunset. After the sun goes down, families gather at home for a light meal before bed. The next morning, Muslims get up around 3:00 or 4:00 A.M. to eat breakfast before sunrise. At 7:00 A.M. on the last day of Ramadan, families dress in new clothes and go to their mosque (house of worship) to pray.

The celebration of Eid al-Fitr ends the Ramadan fast. The party lasts for three days. Most Muslims don't work during this time. People dress up in new clothes and exchange gifts with family and friends. Muslims enjoy a big meal of rice, cake, orange juice, *sampus* (beef turnovers), and halwud. Families who can afford to slaughter goats, camels, or cows for the feast. But most Muslims add just a little lamb to rice to make *skudahkharis,* a thick stew. In Tanzania, cooks mix green plantains with chicken broth to make *supa ya ndizi,* East African plantain soup. They usually eat this nourishing soup with a rice and fish dish called *wali na samaki.*

On August 12, East African Muslims celebrate Molit, the day Muhammad was born, got married, and died. They honor Muhammad by taking the day off from work to pray and fast. At nightfall, families gather to eat a meal of rice, roasted goat, tea, and orange juice. Adults read from the Koran (the holy book of Islam) and give children gifts and money.

Half of all Kenyans follow either Islam or traditional religions— age-old belief systems that teach that spirits live within rocks, trees, and animals. Harvest festivals and planting celebrations honor these spirits and give thanks for the rain and sunshine needed to make the crops grow. In April, the Masai and other ethnic groups in southern Kenya celebrate the beginning of the rainy season. This is the time of year when southern Kenyans move their cattle to the fresh green grass and clear streams of the Great Rift Valley. For several days, the Masai feast, sing, and pray that their cattle remain healthy. Dancers in colorful costumes and musicians who play handmade drums and flutes entertain the festivalgoers.

Many Kenyans are Christians who celebrate Christian holidays such as Christmas and Easter. Kenya, like many of the countries in East Africa, was once a British colony. For this reason, a Kenyan Christmas follows many of the same traditions honored in Britain, such as giving gifts and decorating a tree. But the holiday feast is

An Ethiopian girls' choir performs during a Christian holiday. About half of Ethiopia's population belong to the Ethiopian Orthodox Church.

more likely to feature fresh fish, sandwiches, vegetables, and fruits than turkey with stuffing.

In Ethiopia, where the population includes both Muslims and Christians, Christmas is celebrated on December 19 in accordance with the Ethiopian calendar. Although Ethiopian kids don't look forward to a visit from Santa Claus, they do decorate a Christmas tree and receive presents from friends and relatives. Ethiopians light candles and listen to Christmas music. Families dress in white cotton robes, handmade for the holiday, and go to church. Christmas dinner features roast lamb, rice, vegetables, and a special holiday bread called *hebyasha*.

Maskal is another Christian holiday celebrated in Ethiopia. Ethiopian Christians believe that in the fourth century A.D., Queen

Women in East African villages are in charge of most farming chores. Here, two villagers in Tanzania work together to plant sweet potatoes.

Helena, Emperor Constantine's mother, traveled to Jerusalem in search of the cross on which Jesus was crucified. She found the cross and lit a huge bonfire to ward off evil spirits. Ethiopians celebrate the Maskal festival with parades that feature marching bands and hundreds of people carrying blazing crosses. After dark, fireworks and bonfires light up the night. People dance, sing, and feast on roasted lamb, spicy stews called *wats*, and *injera*, a flat bread.

More than half of Uganda's population is Christian. But those who practice traditional religions often participate in Christian celebrations and vice versa. A Christian priest or minister will usually lead the people in prayer and then traditional performers will dance to communicate with the spirits and ancestors. Food is a part of every festival. Fresh fish, caught from one of Uganda's many lakes, is especially popular. No matter what the occasion, East Africans of all backgrounds make the day special with favorite foods.

Before You Begin

Cooking any dish, plain or fancy, is easier and more fun if you are familiar with its ingredients. East African cooking makes use of some ingredients that you may not know. You should also be familiar with the special terms that will be used in various recipes in this book. Therefore, *before* you start cooking any of the dishes in this book, study "The Careful Cook" and the following "dictionary" of special cooking utensils, terms, and ingredients. Then read through each recipe you want to try from beginning to end. Shop for ingredients and organize the cookware you will need. Once you have assembled everything, you can begin to cook.

Samusas (recipe on page 36), a staple of East Africa, can be filled with ground meat or vegetables.

The Careful Cook

Whenever you cook, there are certain safety rules you must always keep in mind. Even experienced cooks follow these rules when they are in the kitchen.

- Always wash your hands before handling food. Thoroughly wash all raw vegetables and fruits to remove dirt, chemicals, and insecticides. Wash uncooked poultry, fish, and meat under cold water before preparing.
- Use a cutting board when cutting up vegetables and fruits. Don't cut them up in your hand! And be sure to cut in a direction *away* from you and your fingers.
- Long hair or loose clothing can easily catch fire if brought near the burners of a stove. If you have long hair, tie it back before you start cooking.
- Turn all pot handles toward the back of the stove so that you will not catch your sleeves or jewelry on them. This is especially important when younger brothers and sisters are around. They could easily knock off a pot and get burned.
- Always use a pot holder to steady hot pots or to take pans out of the oven. Don't use a wet cloth on a hot pan because the steam it produces could burn you.
- Lift the lid of a steaming pot with the opening away from you so that you will not get burned.
- If you get burned, hold the burn under cold running water. Do not put grease or butter on it. Cold water helps to take the heat out, but grease or butter will only keep it in.
- If grease or cooking oil catches fire, throw baking soda or salt at the bottom of the flame to put it out. (Water will *not* put out a grease fire.) Call for help, and try to turn all the stove burners to "off."

Cooking Utensils

colander—A bowl with holes in the bottom and sides. It is used for draining liquid from a solid food.

pastry brush—A small brush with nylon bristles used for coating food with melted butter or other liquids

rolling pin—A cylindrical tool used for rolling out dough

skewer—A thin metal or wooden rod used to hold small pieces of food for broiling or grilling

slotted spoon—A spoon with small openings in the bowl. It is used to pick solid food out of a liquid.

spatula—A flat, thin utensil, usually metal, used to lift, toss, turn, or scoop up food

tongs—A utensil shaped either like a scissors or a tweezers with flat, blunt ends used to grasp food

Cooking Terms

brown—To cook food quickly in fat over high heat so that the surface turns an even brown

garnish—To decorate with small pieces of food such as sprigs of parsley

knead—To work dough by pressing it with the palms, pushing it outward, and then pressing it over on itself

sauté—To fry quickly over high heat in oil or fat, stirring or turning the food to prevent burning

simmer—To cook over low heat in liquid kept just below its boiling point. Bubbles may occasionally rise to the surface.

stir-fry—To quickly cook bite-sized pieces of food in a small amount of oil over high heat

Special Ingredients

black-eyed peas—Small, tan peas with a large black spot from which they get their name

bouillon cubes—Small cubes that make meat broth when combined with hot water

cardamom—A spice of the ginger family, used whole or ground, that has a rich aroma and gives food a sweet, cool taste

chili—A small, hot, red or green pepper

cloves—Dried buds from a small evergreen tree, which can be used whole or ground to flavor food

coconut milk—The white, milky liquid extracted from coconut meat, used to give a coconut flavor to foods. It is available at most super-markets.

collard greens—The leaves of a plant related to the cabbage

coriander—An herb used ground or fresh as a flavoring or garnish

cumin—The seeds of an herb used whole or ground to give food a pungent, slightly hot flavor

eggplant—A vegetable with shiny purple-black skin and yellow flesh

egg roll skins—Thin sheets of dough that can be wrapped around a filling and fried

garlic—A bulb-forming herb whose distinctive flavor is used in many dishes. Each bulb can be broken up into sections called cloves. Most recipes use only one or two cloves. Before you chop up a clove of garlic, you will have to remove the papery covering that surrounds it.

ginger root—A knobby, light brown root used to flavor foods

jalapeño pepper—A Mexican hot pepper

mung bean—A bean often used in Asian cooking that is available in Asian grocery stores, co-ops, or specialty stores

paprika—Dried ground sweet red peppers used for their flavor and color

plantain—A starchy fruit that looks like a banana and must be cooked before it is eaten

seasoned salt—A commercially prepared mixture of salt and other seasonings

thyme—A fragrant herb used fresh or dried to season food

turmeric—A yellow, aromatic spice made from the root of the turmeric plant

vermicelli—Pasta made in long, thin strands that are thinner than spaghetti

yeast—An ingredient used in cooking to make bread rise and cause liquid to ferment

Healthy and Low-Fat Cooking Tips

Because East African cooking relies on many vegetables and legumes and not on cream and butter, many dishes are naturally low in fat. You can lower the fat content in many of these dishes even further by eliminating the meat from the recipes. Some of the recipes featured in this book do require deep-frying. If you are particularly concerned about cutting fat from your diet, consider baking these items instead.

In general, there are many things you can do to prepare healthy, low-fat meals. Here are a few general tips for adapting the recipes in this book. Throughout the book, you'll also find specific suggestions for individual recipes—and don't worry, they'll still taste delicious!

Many recipes call for butter or oil to sauté vegetables or other ingredients. Using olive oil or canola oil instead of butter lowers saturated fat right away, but you can also reduce the amount of oil you use—often by half. Sprinkling a little salt on the vegetables brings out their natural juices, so less oil is needed. It's also a good idea to use a small, non-stick frying pan if you decide to use less oil than the recipe calls for. Using cooking sprays such as Pam to grease cooking dishes is an option, too.

Another common substitution for butter is margarine. Before making this substitution, consider the recipe. When desserts call for butter, it's often best to use butter. Margarine may noticeably change the taste or consistency of the food.

For some recipes, you might like to substitute a mixture of evaporated skim milk and shredded coconut in place of coconut milk to lower the fat content. This substitution works well in recipes for soups.

Lower the fat content of egg dishes by using an egg substitute in place of real eggs. When broth is called for, use low-fat and nonfat canned varieties to cut the fat.

There are many ways to prepare meals that are good for you and still taste great. As you become a more experienced cook, try experimenting with recipes and substitutions to find the methods that work best for you.

METRIC CONVERSIONS

Cooks in the United States measure both liquid and solid ingredients using standard containers based on the 8-ounce cup and the tablespoon. These measurements are based on volume, while the metric system of measurement is based on both weight (for solids) and volume (for liquids). To convert from U.S. fluid tablespoons, ounces, quarts, and so forth to metric liters is a straightforward conversion, using the chart below. However, since solids have different weights—one cup of rice does not weigh the same as one cup of grated cheese, for example—many cooks who use the metric system have kitchen scales to weigh different ingredients. The chart below will give you a good starting point for basic conversions to the metric system.

MASS (weight)

1 ounce (oz.)	=	28.0 grams (g)
8 ounces	=	227.0 grams
1 pound (lb.) or 16 ounces	=	0.45 kilograms (kg)
2.2 pounds	=	1.0 kilogram

LIQUID VOLUME

1 teaspoon (tsp.)	=	5.0 milliliters (ml)
1 tablespoon (tbsp.)	=	15.0 milliliters
1 fluid ounce (oz.)	=	30.0 milliliters
1 cup (c.)	=	240 milliliters
1 pint (pt.)	=	480 milliliters
1 quart (qt.)	=	0.95 liters (l)
1 gallon (gal.)	=	3.80 liters

PAN SIZES

8-inch cake pan	=	20 x 4-centimeter cake pan
9-inch cake pan	=	23 x 3.5-centimeter cake pan
11 x 7-inch baking pan	=	28 x 18-centimeter baking pan
13 x 9-inch baking pan	=	32.5 x 23-centimeter baking pan
9 x 5-inch loaf pan	=	23 x 13-centimeter loaf pan
2-quart casserole	=	2-liter casserole

LENGTH

¼ inch (in.)	=	0.6 centimeters (cm)
½ inch	=	1.25 centimeters
1 inch	=	2.5 centimeters

TEMPERATURE

212°F	=	100°C (boiling point of water)
225°F	=	110°C
250°F	=	120°C
275°F	=	135°C
300°F	=	150°C
325°F	=	160°C
350°F	=	180°C
375°F	=	190°C
400°F	=	200°C

(To convert temperature in Fahrenheit to Celsius, subtract 32 and multiply by .56)

An East African Table

Before eating, East Africans wash their hands in a bowl of soapy water placed near the table. Family and friends may dine at a table with chairs, but in small villages, people are just as likely to take a seat on the floor. A typical East African meal features a main dish— usually a thick soup or stew made with vegetables, meat, poultry, or fish—served on individual plates. A starch, such as chapati, is served on a communal plate. The diners break off a piece of chapati and use it to scoop up some of the food on their plate.

Although diners in big city restaurants may use silverware, the traditional way to eat in East Africa is to use the right hand. Dinnertime is a chance for diners to relax, talk, and catch up on the day's news. After a leisurely main course, East Africans might enjoy fruits such as mangoes or plantains for dessert.

Plantains, bananalike fruits that are hard and starchy, are usually cooked before eating. Plantains can be fried (front), boiled with vegetables (back left), or grilled (back right). (Recipes on pages 42–43.)

An East African Menu

East Africans traditionally eat two meals per day, one at noon and one in the evening. The two meals are basically the same. They are usually made up of a soup or stew served with some sort of starch such as chapati or *matoke* (mashed plantains). Desserts are more common in the city than they are in rural villages. Below are two East African dinner menus.

DINNER #1

Chapatis

Samusas

Avocado and papaya salad

Groundnut sauce with rice

Kashata

SHOPPING LIST:

Produce

1 bunch green onions
2 large avocados
1 small papaya
1 red grapefruit
1 small head Bibb lettuce
1 medium onion
2 medium tomatoes
1 small eggplant

Dairy/Egg/Meat

1½ lb. extra-lean ground
beef or 4 fist-sized
potatoes and 1 c. frozen
peas

Canned/Bottled/Boxed

vegetable oil
lemon juice
olive oil
1 bag grated coconut or
½ lb. unsalted peanuts

Miscellaneous

salt
flour
cumin seed
garlic powder
seasoned salt
black pepper
1 package square egg roll
skins
smooth sugar-free peanut
butter
rice
sugar
cinnamon

DINNER #2

Ethiopian flat bread

Greens with coconut milk

East African plantain soup

Fresh steamed fish

Vermicelli and raisins

SHOPPING LIST:

Produce

1 pound fresh collard greens or 1 10-oz. package frozen collard greens
3 medium onions
3 large tomatoes
3 medium tomatoes
2 or 3 green plantains
1 clove garlic

Dairy/Egg/Meat

2 lb. fresh or frozen fish fillets (red snapper, orange roughy, halibut, or cod)

Canned/Bottled/Boxed

club soda
1 can coconut milk
48 oz. canned chicken or vegetable broth
vegetable oil
1 box vermicelli pasta
1 box raisins
1 bag chopped dates
1 bag chopped walnuts

Miscellaneous

self-rising flour
salt
pepper
cardamom
sugar

Staples and Snacks

Mild-flavored staples, such as rice and bread, are natural accompaniments to East Africa's hearty soups, stews, and sauces. These foods are often used as "utensils" to scoop up other foods, and some, such as chapatis, can also be eaten alone as a snack.

East Africans eat many snacks throughout the day. These snacks, which can also be served as appetizers, are usually very nutritious and actually amount to mini-meals.

Rice pancakes (front) and chapatis (back) are popular snacks. The pancakes go well with jam, and the chapatis get an extra kick when sprinkled with a little sugar. (Recipes on pages 32–33.)

Chapatis (Kenya, Tanzania, Uganda)

In Africa, chapatis are considered a luxury, because only those who can afford to buy imported flour can make them.

½ tsp. salt

3 c. unbleached all-purpose flour

¾ c. plus 1 to 3 tbs. vegetable oil

¾ to 1 c. water

1. In a large bowl, combine salt and 2½ c. flour. Add ¾ c. oil and mix well. Add water little by little, stirring after each addition, until dough is soft. Knead dough in bowl for 5 to 10 minutes.

2. Sprinkle about ¼ c. flour on a flat surface. Take a 2-inch ball of dough and, with a floured rolling pin, roll out into a ⅛-inch-thick circle the size of a saucer. Repeat with remaining dough, sprinkling flat surface with flour if dough sticks.

3. Heat 1 tbsp. oil in a large skillet over medium-high heat for 1 minute. Fry chapati 3 to 5 minutes per side or until brown.

4. Remove from pan and let drain on paper towels. Fry remaining chapatis, adding more oil if necessary.

5. Serve immediately or place in a covered container until ready to serve.

Preparation time: 25 minutes
Makes 6 chapatis

Rice Pancakes (Kenya)

1 tbsp. (approximately) active dry yeast

½ to 1 c. warm water (105 to 115°F)

1 c. sugar

2¾ c. rice flour

¼ tsp. ground cardamom

¼ c. canned coconut milk

vegetable oil

Yeast makes these pancakes light and airy. If the yeast does not start to foam after about 5 minutes in warm water, throw it out and try again with new yeast.

1. In a small bowl, dissolve yeast* in ½ c. warm water. Add a pinch of sugar and set aside in a warm place for about 5 minutes or until yeast mixture foams.

2. In a large bowl, combine sugar, flour, and cardamom. Add coconut milk and yeast mixture and stir. Mixture should have the consistency of pancake batter. If too thick, stir in water little by little until batter runs slowly from spoon.

3. Cover bowl with a towel (not terry cloth) and set aside in a warm place for about 1 hour or until mixture nearly doubles in size.

4. Heat 1 tbsp. oil in a large skillet over medium-high heat for 1 minute. Pour ½ c. of batter into pan and spread with a spoon to form a pancake about the size of a saucer. Cover pan and cook pancake for 1 to 2 minutes or until golden brown on bottom. Sprinkle pancake with a few drops of oil and turn over with a spatula. Cover and cook for another 1 to 2 minutes or until golden brown on other side. Repeat with remaining batter, adding more oil when necessary.

Preparation time: 2 hours
Makes about 10 pancakes

Meat on a Stick (Ethiopia, Uganda)

The seasoned meat and onions can also be cooked in a frying pan with a little vegetable oil. In East Africa, the skewered meat is cooked over hot coals.

1 tsp. ground red pepper

1 tsp. garlic powder

½ tsp. seasoned salt

1½ lb. beef tenderloin or round steak, cut into bite-sized pieces

1 medium onion, peeled and cut into 1-inch pieces

1. Combine red pepper, garlic powder, and seasoned salt in a wide, shallow bowl. Add beef pieces and mix with hands to coat meat with spices.

2. Preheat broiler or grill.

3. Thread beef and onion pieces onto eight 12-inch skewers. Broil 4 to 5 minutes per side or until meat is tender.

Preparation time: 20 minutes
Makes 8 skewers

Before grilling the meat in this appetizer, East African cooks cover it with a mixture of ground red pepper, garlic powder, and salt to give it extra zest.

Samusas

This snack, which originated in India, is a favorite in East Africa. In the cities, samusas are sold at street stands.

1½ lb. extra-lean ground beef*

½ tsp. cumin seed

2 tbsp. chopped green onion

dash garlic powder

dash seasoned salt

dash black pepper

¼ c. all-purpose flour

2 tbsp. water (or one egg, beaten)

1 package square egg roll skins

1 c. vegetable oil

1. In a large frying pan, break up the ground beef* with a fork. Add cumin, green onion, garlic powder, seasoned salt, and black pepper and mix well.

2. Brown meat over medium heat. Drain off fat and set aside.

3. In a small bowl, combine flour and 2 tbsp. water (or the beaten egg) and stir to make a paste.

4. Place 1 egg roll skin on a flat surface. Cover remaining skins with a slightly damp kitchen towel (not terry cloth) so they don't dry out. Fill according to directions on page 37.

5. In a large frying pan, heat oil over medium-high heat for 3 to 4 minutes. With tongs, carefully place 1 samusa in oil. Samusa should fry to golden brown in about 3 minutes. If it takes longer than this, increase the temperature of the oil. Remove samusa from oil with slotted spoon and drain on paper towels. Repeat with remaining samusas, frying 3 or 4 at a time.

How to fill samusas:

1. With a pastry brush, brush all 4 edges of skin with flour and water mixture.

2. Place about 1 tbsp. of meat mixture just above center of skin.

3. Fold skin in half over filling to form a triangle and press edges together to seal.

4. Repeat with remaining skins.

Preparation time: 1 hour
Makes about 24 samusas

* To make this a vegetarian dish, replace the ground beef with potatoes and peas. Peel, cut up, and boil 4 fist-sized potatoes. When soft, drain and mash. Mix in 1 c. peas and spices. Fill samusas as instructed.

Fruits and Vegetables

Many varieties of fruits and vegetables grow in East Africa, and they are an important part of East African cooking. What people don't grow in their own gardens, they buy in open-air markets that offer everything from bananas and cucumbers to guavas and yams. These fruit and vegetable dishes can be eaten alone for a snack, a light lunch or supper, or can be served as side dishes.

Avocados, papayas, and grapefruit liven up this fresh fruit salad (recipe on page 40). Open-air markets carry many different types of fruits grown throughout East Africa.

Avocado and Papaya Salad

This salad is popular in Kenya. Although salads were not served on East African tables until colonial times, they have been more common in modern times.

2 large avocados

1 small papaya

1 red grapefruit

1 small head Bibb lettuce

1 tbsp. lemon juice

2 tbsp. olive oil

salt and pepper to taste

1. Slice the avocados and papaya in half. Remove the pits and the seeds. Scoop out the fleshy pulp with a spoon.

2. Cut the fruits into 1-inch pieces and combine them in a medium bowl.

3. Peel the grapefruit and divide it into segments. Peel the thin skin from each segment.

4. Cut each segment in half and add them to the avocado and papaya mix.

5. Wash the lettuce and use paper towel to pat the leaves dry.

6. Arrange the lettuce leaves on a plate. Spoon the fruit mixture on top of the leaves.

7. In a small bowl, use a fork or whisk to combine the lemon juice, olive oil, salt, and pepper.

8. Drizzle the dressing over the salad and serve.

Preparation time: 20 minutes
Serves 4 to 6

Greens with Coconut Milk (Kenya, Uganda)

¾ c. water

1 lb. fresh collard greens,* cleaned and chopped, or 1 10-oz package frozen chopped collard greens, thawed

1 medium onion, peeled and chopped

3 large tomatoes, cubed

1 c. canned coconut milk

dash of salt

1. In a large saucepan, bring water to a boil over high heat. Add collard greens, reduce heat to low, and simmer for 4 to 5 minutes.

2. Add onions, tomatoes, coconut milk, and salt and stir well. Cook, uncovered, 20 minutes more. Serve hot.

Preparation time: 35 minutes
Serves 4 to 6

* Other types of greens, such as spinach, turnip greens, or kale, can be substituted for the collard greens.

Versatile Plantains

Plantains are an important food in East Africa. Although it is a member of the banana family, the plantain is often served as a vegetable. For variety, try adding tomatoes, onions, fresh spinach, or a dash of curry powder to boiled plantains.

Boiled Plantains

2 large, firm, green plantains*

dash salt

butter, to taste

1. Wash and peel the plantains. Cut into 1-inch pieces and place in a large kettle.

2. Cover with water and add salt.

3. Bring to a boil over high heat. Reduce heat to medium-low, cover, and simmer for 10 minutes or until plantains can be easily pierced with a fork. Serve hot with butter.

Preparation time: 10–15 minutes
Serves 4

* Green plantains are not yet fully ripe. They can withstand the boiling process better than yellow (ripe) plantains.

Fried Plantains

3 large, yellow plantains

vegetable oil

1. Wash and peel plantains. Slice into thin rounds.

2. In a large frying pan, heat ¼ inch oil over medium high heat for 4 to 5 minutes.

3. Add plantain slices and fry for 4 to 5 minutes or until golden brown on both sides.

4. Remove from oil with slotted spoon and drain on paper towels.

Preparation time: 10–15 minutes
Serves 4

Grilled Plantains

3 large, yellow plantains

1. Wash the plantains and cut them in half lengthwise and widthwise. Do not peel.

2. Preheat grill or broiler.

3. Grill or broil, skin side down, for 5 to 7 minutes or until plantains can be easily pierced with a fork and aren't sticky.

4. When cool enough to handle, peel plantains and serve.

Preparation time: 10–15 minutes
Serves 4

Sauces and Stews

East African sauces and soups are quite similar to each other. Soups are served with a starch, such as chapatis, on the side for dipping, while sauces, which are thicker than soups, are often served over a starch such as rice. Stews are heartier than soups and sauces and usually make up the main part of the meal.

Groundnut sauce (recipe page 48) uses protein-rich peanut butter as a main ingredient. The dish can be served in place of meat over rice, sweet potatoes, or plantains.

Choroko Sauce (Uganda)

Although the flavor will be different, choroko sauce can also be made with split peas.

1½ c. dried Shirakiku® brand mung beans

2 tbsp. vegetable oil

3 medium tomatoes, cut into bite-sized pieces

1 large onion, peeled and chopped

3 or 4 cloves garlic, peeled and crushed

½ tsp. seasoned salt

dash salt

dash black pepper

½ c. water

1. Place beans in a medium bowl and cover with cold water. Let soak overnight.

2. Drain beans in a colander.

3. Fill a medium saucepan half full of water and bring to a boil over high heat. Add beans and cook for 1 to 1½ hours or until tender.

4. Drain beans in a colander and place in a medium bowl. Mash well with a fork.

5. In a large frying pan, heat oil over medium heat for 1 minute.

6. Add tomatoes, onions, and garlic and sauté until onions are transparent.

7. Add mashed beans, seasoned salt, salt, black pepper, and ½ c. water and simmer for 15 to 20 minutes. Serve over rice or with chapatis.

Soaking time: overnight
Preparation time: 2 hours
Serves 4 to 6

Groundnut Sauce

This sauce is made from groundnuts, better known in some countries as peanuts. Groundnut sauce is often substituted for meat dishes, although it is also served with dried meat and dried fish.

2 tbsp. vegetable oil

1 medium onion, peeled and chopped

2 medium tomatoes, cut into bite-sized pieces

1 small eggplant, with or without peel, cut into bite-sized pieces

½ c. smooth peanut butter*

¼ c. water

1. In a large frying pan, heat oil over medium heat for 1 minute. Add onions and sauté until transparent.

2. Add tomatoes and cook for 5 minutes. Add eggplant and cook for 5 minutes more.

3. In a small bowl, combine peanut butter and ¼ c. water and stir to make a paste. Add to tomato-eggplant mixture and stir well.

4. Reduce heat to medium-low and simmer, uncovered, for 10 minutes or until eggplant is tender.

5. Serve with rice, potatoes, sweet potatoes, or plantains.

Preparation time: 30 minutes
Serves 4 to 6

* This recipe works best if made with natural peanut butter with no sugar added. Check the health food section of your local supermarket.

Banana and Meat Stew

1 lb. beef, cut in cubes

2 c. water

2 onions, sliced

2 tomatoes, peeled and sliced

2 tbsp. oil

2 medium green plantains, or 4 small green bananas, washed, peeled, sliced, and placed in a bowl with cold water

1 c. coconut milk

salt and pepper, to taste

1. Place the meat and water in a pot and simmer for 1 hour.

2. Sauté the onion and tomato in hot oil in a large skillet until the onions are soft and golden.

3. Add cooked meat, plantains or bananas, and coconut milk. If the coconut milk does not cover the meat, add some of the meat stock.

4. Season with salt and pepper. Simmer gently until bananas are cooked and the meat is tender. If you are using regular bananas, add them 15 to 20 minutes before the meat is done.

Preparation time: 1½ hours
Serves 4 to 6

Main Dishes

In East Africa, a thick, hearty stew is likely to be the main dish at nearly every meal. Such dishes feed more people at less cost and may not contain meat at all. On occasion, however, meat, vegetables, and starch may be served separately. Meat-based dishes are not daily fare, because meat is an expensive food item.

Meat curry (recipe on page 53) can be made with chicken, lamb, or goat.

Luku (Ethiopia)

Because of the high cost of chicken in East Africa, luku is usually reserved for special occasions.

8 hard-boiled eggs*

¾ c. vegetable oil

5 to 6 c. chopped onion

¼ c. tomato paste

½ c. water

2 tsp. salt

¾ tsp. black pepper

1 tbsp. finely chopped garlic

2 tsp. paprika

¼ tsp. ground cumin (optional)

8 pieces chicken,
    rinsed and patted dry

1. Remove shells from hard-boiled eggs while still warm. With a sharp knife, make 4 to 5 shallow cuts on both sides of each egg. Set aside.

2. In a large kettle, heat 2 tbsp. oil over medium-high heat for 1 minute. Add onions and sauté for 8 to 10 minutes or until onions start to turn brown.

3. Reduce heat to medium and add tomato paste and ½ c. water. Stir well. Cook for 10 minutes, then add remaining oil. Cook for 5 minutes more.

4. Add salt, black pepper, garlic, paprika, cumin, and chicken. Reduce heat to low and simmer, uncovered, for about 30 minutes.

5. Add eggs, cover, and cook for 10 minutes or until chicken is tender.

Preparation time: 1 hour and 15 minutes
Serves 6

* To make hard-boiled eggs, place the eggs in a pan and cover with cold water. Bring to a boil and cook for 15 to 20 minutes.

Meat Curry

½ c. vegetable oil

½ c. plus 2 tbsp. chopped onion

4 cloves garlic, peeled and finely chopped

1 1-inch piece ginger root, peeled and chopped

2 tsp. cumin seed

4 whole cardamom pods

1 2- to 3-inch cinnamon stick

4 whole cloves

½ tsp. ground red pepper

1 tsp. turmeric powder

1 6-oz. can tomato paste

4 to 6 pieces chicken, rinsed and patted dry

2 medium white potatoes, peeled and quartered

½ c. fresh coriander

1. In a large frying pan, heat oil over medium heat for 1 minute. Add onion, garlic, ginger root, cumin, cardamom, cinnamon stick, cloves, red pepper, and turmeric and stir.

2. Stir in tomato paste and cook about 10 minutes or until tomato paste separates from oil. Stir to blend oil and tomato paste.

3. Add chicken, reduce heat to low, and cover. Simmer for 35 minutes.

4. Add potatoes, cover, and simmer 15 minutes or until tender.

5. Add coriander and simmer, uncovered, 10 minutes more.

Preparation time: 1 hour and 15 minutes
Serves 4 to 6

Fresh Steamed Fish (Uganda)

In East Africa, this dish is made with a whole fish, with or without the head. This recipe works well with red snapper or orange roughy.

¼ c. vegetable oil

2 medium onions, peeled and chopped

1 clove garlic, peeled and chopped

3 medium tomatoes, chopped

½ tsp. salt

¼ tsp. black pepper

2 lb. fish fillets

1. In a large frying pan, heat oil over medium heat for 1 minute. Add onions and sauté until transparent.

2. Add garlic, tomatoes, salt, and black pepper and mix well.

3. Place fish in the center of tomato mixture. Cover and simmer for about 25 minutes or until fish is tender and flaky.

Preparation time: 45 minutes
Serves 4 to 6

Tomatoes from the open-air market and freshly caught fish make this East African dish even more appetizing.

Vegetable Casserole (Uganda)

The variations of this colorful vegetable casserole are endless. Either make it with the vegetables listed here or substitute your own favorites.

2 tbsp. vegetable oil

I small onion, sliced and separated into rings

I medium eggplant, unpeeled, cut into bite-sized pieces

I small sweet red pepper, cored and thinly sliced

I or 2 cloves garlic, peeled and crushed

I lb. fresh spinach, cleaned and chopped, or I 10-oz. package frozen chopped spinach, thawed

I small zucchini, peeled and sliced

2 medium tomatoes, cut in wedges

½ tsp. salt

¼ tsp. black pepper

1. In a large frying pan, heat oil over medium-high heat for 1 to 2 minutes.

2. Add onions to pan and stir-fry for 2 to 3 minutes. Continue to add vegetables to pan in order listed, stir-frying each 2 to 3 minutes before adding the next.

3. Stir in salt and black pepper. Cover pan, reduce heat to low, and simmer 10 to 15 minutes or until vegetables are tender.

4. Serve immediately.

Preparation time: 45 minutes
Serves 4 to 6

Pilau

For variety, you can add other vegetables, such as cabbage, carrots, or green beans, to this popular rice dish originally from India.

2 tbsp. butter or oil

2 large onions, chopped

2 cloves garlic, crushed

1 lb. lean beef,* cut into 1½-inch cubes

2 tomatoes, peeled and sliced

1 c. water

2 c. coconut milk

1 c. rice

½ tsp. cardamom seeds

1 stick cinnamon

2 tsp. salt

1½ tsp. lemon juice

1 tsp. oil or melted butter

1. Heat 2 tbsp. of butter or oil in a heavy skillet.

2. Add the onions and garlic and sauté until golden.

3. Mix in the meat and tomatoes and cook, stirring constantly, until the meat begins to brown.

4. Add 1 c. water and simmer for 20 to 30 minutes.

5. Add the coconut milk, rice, spices, and lemon juice and stir to combine. The water and coconut milk should cover the rice by ½ inch. If they do not, add more water.

6. Cover the pan and simmer until the rice is tender (about 20 to 25 minutes). Use a fork to stir.

7. Remove from heat and sprinkle with 1 tsp. oil or melted butter.

8. Place uncovered in a 375°F oven for about 20 minutes, or until all the moisture is absorbed.

* To make this a vegetarian dish, omit the meat and add any or all of the additional vegetables suggested above. You may also substitute chicken, fish, or tofu for the beef.

Preparation time: 2 hours
Serves 4 to 6

Desserts

Sweets have not traditionally been part of the East African diet. While there is more interest in desserts than there used to be, an East African meal is still far more likely to be followed by a piece of fresh fruit, such as an orange or a mango, than any sort of cake or pie. The following desserts are typically East African, because none of them is too rich or too sweet.

Small strips of a pasta called vermicelli combine well with raisins, dates, and walnuts in this simple dessert. (Recipe on page 60.)

Vermicelli and Raisins (Kenya)

2 tbsp. vegetable oil

2 c. vermicelli, broken into 1-inch pieces

2 c. hot water

¾ tsp. ground cardamom

¼ c. sugar

¼ c. raisins*

¼ c. chopped dates (optional)

¼ c. chopped walnuts (optional)

1. In a large frying pan, heat oil over medium heat for 1 minute. Add vermicelli and sauté until light brown.

2. Slowly add 2 c. hot water. Stir in cardamom, sugar, raisins, dates, and nuts.

3. Cover, reduce heat to medium low, and simmer, stirring occasionally, for about 10 minutes or until all water is absorbed and vermicelli is tender.

Preparation time: 20 minutes
Serves 4 to 6

*If you leave out the dates and nuts, increase the amount of raisins by ½ c.

Kashata

These sweet treats are popular during holidays throughout East Africa.

⅔ c. sugar

½ tsp. cinnamon

2 c. grated coconut or ½ lb.
  unsalted peanuts, finely chopped

1. In a heavy skillet, heat the sugar until it melts (about 10 to 15 minutes), stirring constantly. The melted sugar will be dark brown and syrupy.

2. Add the cinnamon and the coconut or peanuts.

3. Cook for about 2 minutes, or until the sugar turns light brown.

4. Remove from the heat and let cool.

5. When the mixture is cool enough to handle, form 1-inch balls and place on wax paper until set.

Preparation time: 30 minutes (plus cooling)
Makes about 20 balls

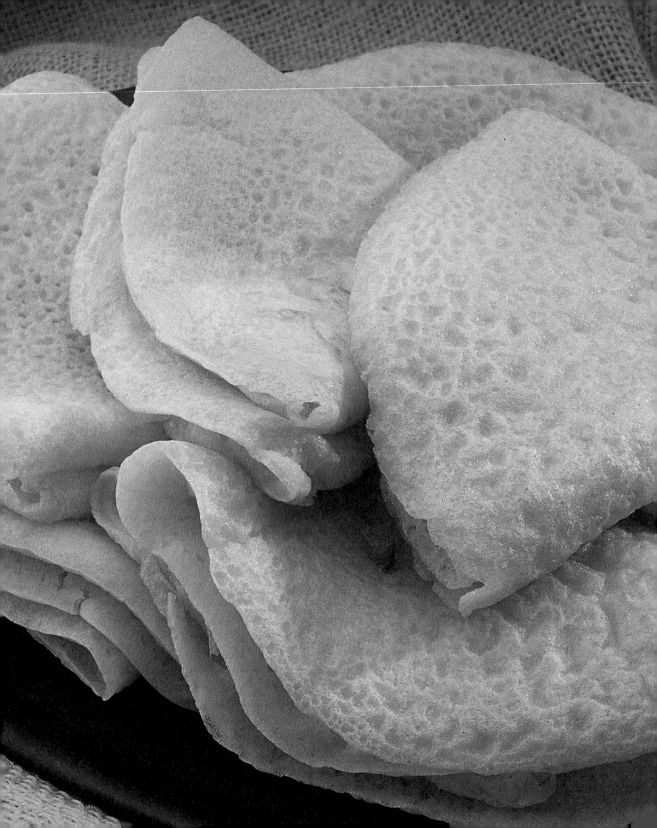

Holiday and Festival Food

The diversity of East Africa's history adds variety to the area's festivals. All of the countries, except Ethiopia (which was never a colony), celebrate achieving independence from European colonial rule. Many of the holidays honor religious events. Islamic, Christian, and traditional observances may prevail, depending on where the celebrations are taking place. No matter what the holiday, local cooks make the day special by preparing favorite foods.

In Ethiopia, injera is the traditional flat bread made from a local grain called teff. The recipe on page 64 uses self-rising flour.

Ethiopian Flat Bread / Injera

This bread, a staple throughout Ethiopia, is often part of the Maskal holiday.

3 c. warm water

2½ c. self-rising flour

3 tbsp. club soda

vegetable oil

1. Pour warm water into a blender or food processor. Add the flour, cover, and blend on low for 10 seconds. Turn blender on high and mix for 30 seconds, until smooth.

2. Pour the batter into a mixing bowl and add the club soda. Mix with a spoon. The batter should have the consistency of heavy cream.

3. Bring a 10-inch skillet to medium heat. Spread ½ tsp. oil over the pan with a pastry brush or paper towel. Use a ladle to pour ½ c. of the batter to one side of the pan. Quickly tilt the pan to spread the batter evenly over the bottom.

4. Small bubbles will soon appear on the surface and the edges of the pancake will curl away from the pan. After 1 minute, use a spatula to remove the injera. Place it on a floursack kitchen towel to cool. The finished injera should be white and easy to bend. Repeat the process until batter is used up.

5. Fold each injera in quarters and stack on a plate to serve.

Preparation time: 30 minutes
Serves 6 to 8

Rice with Fish/Wali na Samaki

Wali na samaki would be served for Eid al-Fitr or Christmas.

2 green bell peppers, seeded and chopped

1 onion, chopped

1 16-oz. can chopped tomatoes

2 c. water

juice of one lemon

1 tsp. grated lemon rind

½ tsp. crushed red pepper, or to taste

3 bay leaves

salt and pepper to taste

2½ to 3 lb. skinless fish fillets such as red snapper, halibut, or cod

1 c. all-purpose flour

vegetable oil

5 to 6 c. cooked rice

1. Combine the first nine ingredients in a Dutch oven. Stir. Over high heat, bring the mixture to a boil.

2. Turn down the heat and simmer the sauce, covered, for about 30 minutes. Remove the bay leaves and keep the sauce warm until ready to serve.

3. Preheat the oven to 200°F. Wash the fish fillets in cold water and pat dry.

4. Pour the flour into a pie pan. Dip the fillets, shaking off the excess flour and placing them on a plate.

5. Heat 2 tbsp. oil in a large skillet over medium-high heat. Add a few of the fish pieces at a time and sprinkle them with salt and pepper. Fry for 3 to 5 minutes on each side, until golden brown.

6. Use a spatula to lift out each fish piece. Transfer the pieces to a baking dish. Keep warm in oven while frying the rest of the fish. Add more oil to the pan as needed.

7. To serve the meal, place a large spoonful of rice on each plate, top with the fish, and then cover with the vegetable sauce.

Preparation time: 1 hour
Serves 6

Lamb and Rice/ Skudahkharis

Somalians often serve this dish to celebrate Eid al-Fitr or other Islamic holidays.

2 tbsp. vegetable oil

1 onion, chopped

1 clove garlic, peeled and minced

1 lb. boneless lamb,* cut into bite-sized pieces

2 tomatoes, chopped

1 tsp. ground cumin

½ tsp. ground cloves

1 tsp. ground cinnamon

½ c. canned tomato paste

5 c. water

2 c. uncooked brown rice

salt and pepper to taste

1. Heat 2 tbsp. oil in a Dutch oven over medium heat. Add the onion, garlic, and lamb. Cook for about 5 minutes, or until the meat is browned, stirring constantly.

2. Add tomatoes, cumin, cloves, cinnamon, tomato paste, and water. Stir to combine.

3. Bring the mixture to a boil over high heat.

4. Add the rice, salt, and pepper. Stir.

5. Reduce the heat to low, and cover the pot. Simmer for 30 minutes or until the rice has absorbed the water.

6. Remove the pot from heat and let stand, covered, for 5 minutes.

7. Serve warm in a large bowl. In Somalia guests eat from the bowl with the fingers of the right hand.

Preparation time: 1 hour
Serves 4

If lamb is not available or is too expensive, you can use beef or chicken instead.

Lentil Salad/ *Yamiser Selatta*

Ethiopian Christians prepare vegetarian main courses, such as this lentil salad, on days when religious practice forbids them to eat meat.

1½ c. dried lentils*

5 c. water

1 onion, chopped

2 tbsp. vinegar

6 tbsp. peanut oil or olive oil

3 cloves garlic, peeled and minced

½ tsp. red pepper flakes

salt and pepper to taste

1. Rinse the lentils in a colander or strainer.

2. In a Dutch oven, cover lentils with 5 c. of water and place on medium heat.

3. Bring to a boil and then lower the heat. Simmer the lentils for 45 minutes or until tender, but not mushy.

4. Carefully pour the lentils into a colander to drain.

5. In a medium bowl, combine the onion, vinegar, oil, garlic, and red pepper flakes.

6. Add the lentils, salt, and pepper.

7. Stir and set aside at room temperature for 1 hour. Stir often to blend flavors.

Preparation time: 2 hours
Serves 6 to 8

*If you are short on time, use canned lentils and ½ c. of bottled Italian dressing.

East African Plantain Soup/ Supa ya Ndizi

This soup is served in Tanzania for Eid al-Fitr.

2 or 3 green plantains, peeled

6 c. canned chicken broth*

salt and pepper to taste

1. Slice the peeled plantains and place in a blender or food processor.

2. Add 1 c. chicken broth and blend until smooth.

3. Pour the mixture into a Dutch oven. Add the remaining 5 c. of broth.

4. Stir to combine. Cover and cook over medium heat for 45 minutes, stirring occasionally.

5. Add salt and pepper to taste.

Preparation time: 1 hour
Serves 4 to 6

*To make this a vegetarian dish, substitute vegetable broth for the chicken broth.

Index

About the Authors

Bertha Vining Montgomery grew up in Social Circle, Georgia. She graduated from Spelman College in Georgia with a B.S. in home economics. Montgomery has taught in all areas of home economics at both the junior and senior high school levels. She would like to thank Janet Clemetson, Farha Ibrahim, the Lawal family, Rukiya Mahmood, and Uche Iheagwara for their help and encouragement with this book.

Constance Nabwire was born and raised in Uganda. She attended King's College Budo in Uganda before coming to the United States on the African Student Program for American Universities. After earning a B.A. in sociology and psychology from Spelman College in Georgia, Nabwire attended the University of Minnesota on a fellowship by the American Association of University Women and graduated with an M.A. in social work. Nabwire has also published several short stories and articles about her native land. Nabwire would like to thank her friends, who contributed their ideas and recipes to this book.

Photo Acknowledgments

The photographs in this book are reproduced courtesy of: © Joe McDonald/Visuals Unlimited, pp. 2–3; © Robert L. & Diane Wolfe, pp. 4 (left and right), 5 (left), 6, 26, 30, 35, 44, 47, 50, 55; © Louiseann and Walter Pietrowicz/September 8th Stock, pp. 5 (right), 18, 38, 58, 62, 67; American Lutheran Church used by permission of Augsburg Fortress, pp. 11, 15; © Glenn Oliver/Visuals Unlimited, p. 12; Phil Porter, p. 16.

Cover photos: © Robert L. & Diane Wolfe, front (top); © Louiseann and Walter Pietrowicz/September 8th Stock, front (bottom), spine, back.

The illustrations on pages 7, 19, 27, 31, 33, 37, 39, 41, 42, 45, 48, 51, 52, 57, 59, 60, 63, 66, 68, and 69 and the map on page 8 are by Tim Seeley.

Lincoln Township Library
2099 W. John Beers Rd.
Stevensville, MI 49127
429-9575